PADRE PIO

A HOLY PRIEST

by
Jim Gallagher

All booklets are published thanks to the
generous support of the members of the
Catholic Truth Society

CATHOLIC TRUTH SOCIETY
PUBLISHERS TO THE HOLY SEE

CONTENTS

Introduction 3

Early Life 7

Ordination 21

Conscripted 31

Padre Pio the Confessor 42

Home for the Relief of Suffering 57

PILGRIMAGE SHRINE

The Shrine 72
   San Giovanni Rotondo 72

Further Information 80

INTRODUCTION

On 1st November, the Feast of All Saints, 1995, Consiglia de Martino dropped her daughter off at school in Salerno and was on her way to Mass.

She felt increasingly ill and before she could even make it to church, stopped at her sister's house. She felt a painful swelling in her neck and when she looked in the mirror saw that it was the size of a grapefruit. Consiglia and her sister became quite frightened. They phoned their husbands to come with them to the hospital.

As soon as a doctor had examined the 43 year-old mother of three, he sent her to the emergency room. A CAT-scan revealed a liquid deposit on the left side of her neck. After a second scan the doctors came up with the diagnosis: a diffuse lymphatic spilling of approximately two litres caused by a rupture of the lymphatic canals. Surgical intervention was advised.

Consiglia and her family were devotees of Padre Pio and she was a member of a Padre Pio prayer group. At the hospital she used her mobile phone to call a Capuchin brother at the friary where Padre Pio had lived in San Giovanni Rotondo. Consiglia was used to making a monthly pilgrimage there to pray at the Padre's tomb.

Consiglia's husband and daughter also called the friar, who later testified that he did in fact go to the Padre's tomb and ask him to intercede for Consiglia.

The next day there was reduction of the fluid deposit in her neck and Consiglia noticed a great decrease in the pain she had been suffering. Examination on the 3rd November showed that the swelling in her neck was almost all gone. An X-ray and examination showed no more evidence of unusual liquid in the system. On 6th November another CAT-scan confirmed the complete disappearance of the liquid deposits.

Consiglia was discharged with a clean bill of health. Subsequent examinations showed no after-effects of the illness.

An investigation at diocesan level lasted almost one year. In September 1997 it was passed to the Congregation for the Causes of Saints, in Rome. A further panel of medical experts unanimously announced the following year the "extraordinary and scientifically inexplicable" nature of Consiglia's cure.

In 1998 at the Vatican the Special Congress of Theologians met to discuss the theological aspects of the healing and later that year the Ordinary Session of Cardinals and Bishops met to discuss the case. On 21st December 1998, in the presence of Pope John Paul II, the Congregation for the Causes of Saints published the decree accepting Consiglia's healing as a miracle attributed to Padre Pio's intercession.

Consiglia was present in St Peter's Square when Pope

John Paul II declared Padre Pio of Pietrelcina Blessed on Sunday 2nd May 1999.

Countless people have tales to tell of the power of the Italian priest's prayers. The Vice-Postulator of the Cause for Padre Pio's Canonisation, Father Gerardo Di Flumeri, presented another healing to the appropriate authorities to consider.

He says, "In the month of February 2000, in the hospital 'The Home for the Relief of Suffering' in San Giovanni Rotondo, a boy of eight years of age was cured from Meningitis Meningoccica with CID. The cure which was extraordinary was attributed to the intercession of Blessed Padre Pio who was invoked in prayer by the boy's parents."

After all the appropriate enquiries and procedures at diocesan and Vatican level, the Holy Father announced on 26th February 2002 that he would Canonise Padre Pio on 16th June 2002.

In an age of multi-national business and the culture of 'enterprise' and 'success', in a time of instant satellite communication, 24-hour entertainment, space travel and new inventions, why do increasing numbers of people throughout the world, particularly young people, exhibit a fascination with and admiration for a Franciscan friar from a little village who lived and died in a remote mountain-top friary in southern Italy?

Padre Pio lived the Catholic priesthood day in and day out for over fifty years in a small Franciscan friary at San

Giovanni Rotondo in southern Italy. His daily agenda was the Divine Office, the Holy Sacrifice of the Mass, community life with his brethren and the priestly ministry of Confession. Hour after hour, day after day he spent cooped up in the confessional. And, from near and far, the people flocked to him.

Padre Pio writing, his pierced hands covered by fingerless mittens.

Early Life

The man who became Padre Pio was born on 25th May 1887 the fourth of eight children to Giuseppa de Nunzio and Grazio Forgione, a peasant couple living in the village of Pietrelcina, about six kilometres from the city of Benevento in southern Italy. He was baptised Francesco, and would be known to his family and friends as 'Franci'.

The family farmed a little land, reckoned to total about five acres, over two or three small fields. They lived in a small stone house in the village and would walk from there to the fields to tend their crops and a few livestock. They were simple peasant farming folk, and people of strong faith. In later life Padre Pio would remark on the goodness of such simple people and lament with tears in his eyes that we would never see their likes again.

Franci's early life was outwardly normal, no signs of anything extraordinary or miraculous. His childhood friends recalled that he played with them and was like them - except that he would never use bad language and, as he had been taught, fled the company if such ever arose. One friend, Luigi Orlando, later recalled that as boys they used to play together and look after their families' sheep in the fields on top of a hill called Piana Romana outside the village. They would have typical boyhood contests of strength. "Francesco nearly always beat me because he was bigger than me. Once, while we were wrestling, we fell and he pinned my shoulders to the ground. In the attempt to turn him and thus reverse the situation, all my efforts were in vain, and so a strong expression escaped my lips. Franci's reaction was immediate; he disengaged himself, got up and ran away all at once because he never, ever said bad words and he didn't want to hear them either."

When he was almost nine years old, in the spring of 1896, his mother took Franci to visit a relative in hospital in Benevento. After the visit Giuseppa took Franci through the wards to visit other patients, stopping here and there for a kindly word, and sometimes a prayer. They stopped at the bed of a young man, a wounded soldier returned from Ethiopia, who was being attended by a nurse and a priest. Franci later remembered that the man "suddenly bowed his head; he remained stock still; and after a few minutes, he died."

Vocation

In August of that year Franci's maternal grandfather died. Later that same year, after hearing an inspiring sermon in church, he told his parents he wanted to be a priest. A year later, in the autumn of 1897, Franci met Brother Camillus from the Capuchin friary at Marcone, who had come to visit Pietrelcina. As he made his way through the village, the friar distributed medals, holy pictures and chestnuts to the children who gathered around him. They were all struck by his cheerfulness and Franci was impressed by his long black bushy beard!

Franci decided there and then that he wanted to be a Capuchin. When his parents said that they would much prefer that he become a secular parish priest, he insisted, "I want to be a friar with a beard"!

Educational opportunities at that time in that place were extremely limited. Franci would need to reach a certain standard before he would ever be accepted for either junior seminary or novitiate. His parents promised him they would find the money to pay for his education and Grazio went abroad, first to Brazil and then to the United States, to work and send money home. Franci's elder brother Michele would eventually join their father to work in America.

At the age of eleven, as was customary - it was the time before Pope St. Pius X lowered the age for children's first Holy Communion - Franci made his first Confession and received his first Holy Communion. Later that same year of 1899 he was confirmed by the Bishop of Benevento in the parish church at Pietrelcina.

While his father worked abroad, his mother oversaw her son's education at home, enrolling him in a private school run in the village. By the age of thirteen his primary education was completed. Giuseppa then found a teacher who taught in the State schools of the region and ran his own private classes in the evening. Thus Franci received two years of secondary education.

A rich interior life

It is recorded that Franci attended Mass every morning, often acting as altar server. The parish priest, Don Pannullo, remained a life-long friend.

While Franci lived a normal, outward, everyday life like everyone else in the village, only later did it become apparent that he had a very rich interior life and intimacy with Our Lord. Much later, Father Agostino, who became his confessor in religious life, wrote in his diary: "The apparitions and ecstasies began at the age of five when he first had the idea of consecrating himself forever to the Lord, and they were continuous. When asked why he had kept them hidden for so long (until 1915), he candidly replied that he had not disclosed them as he believed they were ordinary things which happened to all souls. In fact, one day he naively said, 'Don't you see Our Lady?' To my negative reply he added, 'You only say that out of holy humility.'

But with consolations there also came a spiritual battle, one which Franci Forgione would fight for the rest of his life. For Fr Agostino continued in his diary, "At the age of five the diabolical apparitions began also, and for almost twenty years they were always in the most obscene forms; human and above all bestial."

In the summer of 1902, now aged 15 and having completed his basic secondary education, Franci was able to apply for admission to the Capuchin Order. Sometime that autumn a letter arrived from the Capuchin Father

Provincial saying that he would be accepted into the Order and giving him a date to arrive at the friary of Morcone.

Spiritual battle

It was while he was making final preparations for entry into religious life that Franci had a vision which would reveal to him the mission of spiritual battle which would be the mark of his religious life and his priesthood.

From his own words, from notes written under obedience later in religious life, we have a picture of what the young Franci saw. While he was eager to embrace the penitential life of a Capuchin friar, he was also dreading the day he would have to bid farewell to his beloved mother and other relatives. He was "meditating on his vocation" and wondering how he could steel himself for the new life which lay ahead, above all the departure from his beloved family and Pietrelcina.

"My senses were suddenly suspended and I was made to gaze with the eyes of my intellect on things quite different from those seen by bodily eyes." What he saw was a radiant and majestic figure standing next to him. The man took Franci by the hand and said, "Come with me, for it is fitting that you fight as a valiant warrior." The figure led him to a vast plain where he saw two enormous crowds of people. On the one side they were beautiful and dressed in snow-white, on the other they were all in black and of hideous appearance. These two crowds were separated by a wide gulf into which Franci saw himself placed by his guide.

Suddenly a giant man appeared, "so tall that his forehead touched the clouds, while his countenance was that of a hideous monster."

Franci felt himself go weak and thought he would pass out at the sight. The figure started to advance towards him, while his guide explained that Franci would have to fight this monster. As his knees started to buckle, he begged his guide not to have to fight the ogre. The words the guide replied must have struck into Franci's soul for in his note years later, he puts them in inverted commas, quoting directly: "All resistance is useless; it is advisable that you fight this man. Take heart; enter confidently into the combat, go forward courageously, for I shall be close to you. I will assist you and will not allow him to overcome you. In reward for your victory over him, I shall give you a splendid crown to adorn your head."

These words are the key to the whole of the rest of Francesco Forgione's life. He would end up living in a mountain-top friary in the vicinity of an ancient place of pilgrimage to St Michael the Archangel. As Padre Pio he would, as St Paul instructed us, "fight the good fight" to the end (cf Ephesians 6:10-13). While, as the Church assures us, he is now bathed in the glory of the elect in Heaven, when on earth he shared the sufferings of Our Lord. Many were the people who even saw him suffer from an apparent crown of thorns while he offered the holy Sacrifice of the Mass.

Understandably frightened by the experience but also reassured (the radiant guide had assured him: "Don't be afraid of his attacks or his dreadful aspect. Remember what I have promised you; that I'll always be close to you and help you so that you'll always succeed in overcoming him.") Franci's resolve to enter religious life was strengthened and from that moment never wavered.

Entry to the Friary

Entry to the friary at Morcone was set for 6th January 1903. On New Year's Day, after receiving Holy Communion at Mass, Franci understood that in the vision he had had, the two groups represented the demons and the angels and that the guide was "Jesus Christ Himself" who would always be at his side to assist him in this fight provided he "placed his trust in Him alone and fought generously."

Franci Forgione, later Padre Pio, fought generously to the very end.

While his resolve to quit the world and enter the service of Our Lord in religious life was clear, strong and unambiguous, Franci remained - and would do so throughout his life - extremely affectionate and tender-hearted. His leave-taking of his mother and family (his father still being at work in America) was heartbreaking. While the grief of his departure from loved ones made him feel "that his very bones were being crushed", as the horse and cart arrived to take him and two other boys from the village off to the friary at Morcone, Franci - for the sake of his mother and the others - managed to "shed not a single tear at this painful leave-taking."

On his arrival at the Capuchin novitiate at Morcone, Franci was delighted when the door was opened by Brother Camillus, the friar who had first attracted him to the Franciscan life. The big burly brother threw his arms around the boy, "Bravo Franci, bravo. You've been faithful to the calling and promise of St Francis. Bravo, Franci!"

After a welcome and allocation to their individual cells, the aspirants to religious life embarked on a silent retreat. On 22nd January they were clothed with the religious habit and Franci Forgione become Brother Pio. As Italians celebrate their Name Day more so than their birthday, in later life Padre Pio observed 5th May as his Name Day. That is the feast of Pope St Pius V, sometimes known as 'the Rosary Pope'. It was he who had ordered that the Rosary be said which resulted in the victory of the Papal forces over the Turks in the Battle of Lepanto in 1576.

Franciscan Life

The regime of the Capuchins was an austere one. The day began at midnight with the recitation in the chapel of the offices of Matins and Lauds. The friars would return to their cells for a short sleep before rising again for community prayers at five am. Thus the day proceeded; offices in choir, Holy Mass, manual work and study. The main meal was at mid-day.

While Padre Pio threw himself into the discipline of the Capuchin life, and loved the study of Sacred Scripture, the Franciscan Rule, the mystical theology of St Teresa of Avila and St John of the Cross, he was never glum or downcast. At the appointed times of community recreation when the normal Rule of Silence was lifted, he loved to laugh and joke with his fellow novices. When, once as a Capuchin student, he was sent home for a short while due to sickness, his brethren sorely missed his presence and company in the friary. They later remembered how joyful they felt upon his return.

In the autumn of that year of his novitiate, 1903, Brother Pio's father, Grazio, came home on a visit from the United States. He was shocked at the gaunt appearance of his son and the toll that the rigorous penitential life seemed to be taking on him. Brother Pio never complained.

On 22nd January 1904 the 16 year-old novice made his first vows of poverty, chastity and obedience. There then began a six-year period of training and preparation for ordination to the priesthood (although in the event, Pio would be ordained early by special dispensation). Throughout this period, the students spent time at different houses of the Capuchin province, according to where their teachers of different specialities were based.

San Giovanni Rotondo

Once, during their period of theological studies, at the friary of San Marco la Catola, probably in 1907, the students were discussing the different friaries of the province. One wondered whether the old friary at San Giovanni Rotondo, would ever be re-opened. It had been founded as one of the first Capuchin friaries, just twelve years after Pope Clement VIII had given the Bull for the reform of the Franciscans in 1528. It had, however, been closed since the dissolution of religious orders in Italy in 1866.

One brother remarked that if it ever re-opened he would like to be posted there, with its ideal setting in the Gargano Mountains, the pure air, the remoteness and poverty of the region. The students began jokingly vying with each other as to who should be posted there. They were silenced when Brother Pio coolly and calmly stated that yes, that friary would one day be re-opened but it was he who would be posted there. He said it with such cool conviction that the others were somewhat stunned and moved the conversation on to another topic!

In 1904 when the Father General of the Order had visited the Foggia province, Brother Pio had volunteered to be sent on the foreign missions after his ordination. Because he was already not in the best of health, Fr General turned down this request. As it would turn out, Father Pio would conduct the most intense priestly mission from a remote mountain friary and people from all over the world would flock to be near this man of God.

Bilocation

A mystical phenomenon which would come to be associated with Padre Pio made its first appearance during his student years. Throughout his adult life there would be numerous testimonies from people saying they had seen Padre Pio in different places when, in fact, it was known and witnessed that he was still present in his friary. It is a phenomenon known as bilocation, being present in two places at the same time.

In his religious life as a Capuchin and as a priest, it is said that Padre Pio experienced all the gifts of the Holy Spirit. So united was he with the Heart of our Redeemer and - after the example of Our Lady, Spouse of the Paraclete - so open was he to the workings of the Holy Spirit in him that he appeared to exercise all the charisms of that same Spirit.

In a signed deposition, Brother Pio himself described how on 18th January 1905, while physically present in the friary chapel, along with another brother, he 'suddenly found himself' in a house far away where a man was dying and a little girl was being born to his wife. Our Lady appeared to Pio and told her she was entrusting this little girl to his spiritual care. Eighteen years later, that girl, Giovanna Rizzani, would travel to San Giovanni Rotondo to meet the, by then, already famous Padre Pio. But, to her amazement, she would discover that it was not in fact the first time they had met! In the summer of 1922, when Giovanna was 17, she was visiting St Peter's Basilica in Rome along with a friend. She had some doubts about the Faith and wanted to speak to a priest. She went to a friar sitting in one of the many confessionals in the basilica and very clearly and simply he resolved her questions.

A year later Giovanna heard about Padre Pio and decided to visit San Giovanni Rotondo. Out of all the people waiting to greet him and kiss his hand, Padre Pio immediately singled out Giovanna and walked straight up to her. "I know you," he said. "You were born the night your father died." Giovanna didn't know how the young priest could know this about her.

The next day she went to Confession to him. Pio said to her, "My child, I have waited all these years for you."

Giovanna thought he must be confusing her with someone else and said as much. Pio asked her, "Don't you remember looking for a confessor in St Peter's?" He told her he had gone there in bilocation to hear her confession that day!

Giovanna became a spiritual daughter of Padre Pio and would have an extraordinary experience upon his death 45 years later.

Throughout his life, there came to be many tales of Padre Pio bilocating. Blessed Don Orione told how he saw Padre Pio present in St Peter's Basilica at the Canonisation of Don Bosco in 1934. A bishop said he had seen him present at the Canonisation of St Therese of Lisieux in 1925. All this despite the fact that from the moment of his posting to San Giovanni Rotondo in 1918, Padre Pio never left there. Indeed, he only ever left the friary on a handful of occasions, such as to cast his vote or to visit the hospital he built alongside the friary.

Illness

While continuing his studies for the priesthood, Brother Pio made his final profession as a Capuchin friar on 27th January 1907. During this period he began to experience periods when he could not retain any food. Along with this he would have a racking cough and extremely high temperatures. The community brought in a doctor who diagnosed active tuberculosis. A few months later, having been sent home to Pietrelcina to recuperate, a chest specialist in Naples diagnosed chronic bronchitis, aggravated by Pio's ascetic lifestyle.

Those three elements of his physical state would persist throughout his life. He continued to have bronchitis and also asthma. This must have caused him agonies during the stifling summer heat in the south of Italy when he spent hour after hour in the dark confined space of the confessional. Eating became a penance to him. For great periods he could eat nothing at all.

Eventually, at San Giovanni Rotondo, his superior ordered that he should attend refectory with the community at midday and eat something. Doctors testified that he existed on barely 100 calories a day. Pio once confided that the greatest gift he could receive would to be dispensed from this obedience forcing him to eat something. It truly was a penance for him. There have been other cases of chosen souls who live such a degree of union with Christ, that the physical body is taken into and affected by such union. In recent times, Marthe Robin in France (died 1981) lived for 53 years consuming nothing more than the Holy Eucharist.

And there were the high temperatures. On occasion Pio could even joke about it. For if they did not use a bath thermometer to measure his temperature, the mercury would simply shoot right through the end of a normal one!

ORDINATION

During the period 1909-1916 Pio lived mostly at home in Pietrelcina. His health had broken down completely at the end of 1908 and he was unable to retain any food whatsoever. The Order gave him permission to continue his studies at home. Pio would also feel an incredible heat in his chest as if his heart were on fire and about to burst out of his chest. Again, this was not simply spiritual or metaphorical; he wrote more than once that not even plunging himself into icy cold water was enough to quench the burning heat in his heart.

He had been ordained deacon in January 1909 and it was in May of that year, that he had been given authority to continue his studies at home in Pietrelcina. He was instructed there in the rubrics of the Mass by his old friend Don Pannullo. As his health continued to deteriorate, Pio begged his superiors to allow him to be ordained as soon as possible so that he could at least die as a priest. According to Canon Law, the minimum age for ordination to the priesthood was 24. Fr Benedetto was able to inform him in July 1910 that a special dispensation had been obtained and that at the age of 23, Pio would be ordained the following month.

On the morning of 10th August 1910, he set off with Don Pannullo for Benevento. There, in the Canons' chapel of the cathedral, he was ordained by the 83 year-old archbishop. On the 15th August he returned to Pietrelcina to sing his first public Mass for the feast of the Assumption of Our Blessed Lady into Heaven.

Pio had prepared a little memento card. It bore the words: "A souvenir of my first Mass. Jesus, my life and my breath, today I timorously raise Thee in a mystery of love. With Thee may I be for the world the way, the truth and the life, and through Thee, a holy priest, a perfect victim."

In those words the 23 year-old priest had summed up the whole theology of the Catholic priesthood. Thenceforth he would be completely identified with his Lord and Master, whose priest he was. When he administered the Sacraments of Holy Mother Church, he would act not just as a representative of Christ, but as Christ himself, "in persona Christi".

Christ was and is not only the Great High Priest, but also the Sacrificial Victim (cf Hebrews 7:27; 10:10), whose one eternal sacrifice is offered to the Father each time a priest offers the Holy Mass. Christ Priest and Victim. Padre Pio, faithful son of the Church and priest of Christ, would live to the full his vocation too as both priest and victim.

Stigmata

Less than a month after his ordination, on the afternoon of 7th September 1910, Padre Pio went to see Don Pannullo. He showed him his hands which both had puncture marks in them. He told the parish priest that he had been praying under an elm tree at Piana Romana when Jesus and Mary appeared to him and gave him these wounds.

Don Pannullo sent him to a doctor, who diagnosed tuberculosis of the skin. Another doctor dismissed this diagnosis but could not give any other one. He did note that the wounds were about half an inch in diameter on both sides of the hands, and while they did not bleed, they seemed to go right through the hands from one side to the other.

Padre Pio's mother, Giuseppa, remembered how her son came into the house shaking his hands as if he had just burned himself. She even made a joke out of it: "What's the matter with you? You look like you're trying to play the guitar or something!" Pio said that it was nothing, just that he felt a heat in his hands. Giuseppa noticed, however, that over the next few days he tried to keep his hands hidden.

When the wounds persisted, after a few days Pio went back again to see Don Pannullo. He asked the older priest to pray with him that the Lord would take away the visible signs, although he did not mind suffering the pain of them invisibly. The two priests prayed and the wounds did disappear, although they were to reappear again briefly exactly a year later. Don Pannullo wrote an account of all this which he later sent to the Vatican.

At home in Pietrelcina

Still suffering from ill-health and the inability to retain food, Pio continued to live at home in Pietrelcina. He organised a boys' choir in the local church, the parish of St Anne. He taught religious education to the children of the area. Literacy was low in the area and Padre Pio organised and taught adult literacy classes for the workers in the fields after they had finished work.

During this time Padre Pio continued to feel a call in his soul to identify himself ever-closer to his Lord and Saviour. On the feast of St Michael the Archangel, 29th September 1910, he wrote to his spiritual director, Fr Benedetto: "This desire has been growing continually in my heart and has now become what I would call a strong passion. I have, in fact, made this offering to the Lord several times, beseeching him to pour out on me the punishments prepared for sinners and for souls in a state of purgation, even increasing them a hundredfold.... but I would now like to make this offering to the Lord in obedience to you..."

Fr Benedetto wrote back: "Make the offering of which you speak and it will be most acceptable to the Lord."

Attacks from the Devil

While we have read that even from the age of five, Pio had suffered attacks from the Devil, during this time spent at home in the early days of his priesthood, these became particularly noticeable. Pio continued his ascetic lifestyle, sleeping on the floor with a stone block for a pillow. Sounds of chains and beatings could sometimes be heard during the night. The young priest took to sleeping (or spending the night, for it seems that just as he was no longer eating, he slept very little if at all) in a room the family had in another building known as 'the tower' in Pietrelcina. In summertime he would often spend the night in the hut beside the family's fields on Piana Romana. From both of those places when Pio was there, passers-by or the curious (local children were sometimes particularly curious!) could hear eerie noises and sounds of chains, beatings and of things being thrown around.

Some years later Pio's brother Michele wrote to him to complain that the noises of pots and pans being thrown around during the night still emanated from the tower room. Pio simply replied that Michele should have the room exorcised. He did, and the noises stopped.

We have Pio's own words describing what used to happen in the tower or in the hut at Piano Romano. In a letter of January 1912 he wrote: "The ogre along with many of his fellows does not cease to beat me. I was about to say to death. This happens every day except on Wednesdays. But my Lord and the other noble visitors and heavenly persons make good all my losses by their frequent visits."

In the same letter he wrote of how he was reliving the Passion of Christ, particularly "from Thursday evening until Saturday".

Throughout the rest of his life it seems that he also suffered the Scourging of Christ on Thursday nights. It is heart-rending to see one of the Padre's nightshirts kept by the Capuchin friars; covered from top to bottom in blood from where his flesh was torn by scourges.

Suffering for the sins of priests

In 1911 his superiors were increasingly concerned about the fact that Padre Pio was still living at home in Pietrelcina; whenever he tried to return to a friary, the moment he crossed the threshold he was struck down ill. A medical examination in Naples in October 1911 produces the conclusion by the doctor that Pio was "hopelessly ill" and that he thought it didn't matter where Pio went now to live out his last days, either at home or in a friary.

Fr Benedetto, by this time having been elected Provincial, decided that if his young confrere were about to die, he would die a Capuchin in a Capuchin friary, and ordered Pio to report to the friary at Venafro, where Pio arrived on 28th October 1911.

It was due to his once again living in community that Pio's extraordinary spiritual experiences could no longer remain secret. The Father Guardian at Venafro and others often witnessed Padre Pio in ecstasy. A local doctor, Doctor Nicola Lombardi, witnessed such ecstasies of Padre Pio at least twice and carried out routine tests such as shining a light on the subject's pupils when he was in this state. Lombardi came to consider Pio's experiences "a supernatural phenomenon" and further wrote: "I consider Padre Pio's experiences, ecstasies."

Some of these ecstasies and conversations with Our Lord concerned priests, including the second one witnessed by Dr Lombardi. In it, Padre Pio saw Jesus suffering because of the sins of priests. "How many abominations took place within Your Sanctuary! My Jesus, pardon! .... Punish me and not the others..."

Now it is becoming clearer that Padre Pio was not only living as a victim, identifying with the Spotless Victim who gave Himself on Calvary, but as a victim particularly in atonement for sinful and unworthy priests.

Fifteen months later, March 1913, in a letter to his confessor Fr Agostino, Pio described another similar vision. Jesus told him, "The ingratitude and sleep of my ministers make my agony more difficult to bear. Alas, how they return my love. What pains me even more is that they add scorn and unbelief to their indifference. How many times I was ready to destroy them, but I was held back by the angels and the souls that love me..."

A time of 'exile'

At Venafro Pio's health again collapsed completely and after five weeks Fr Agostino accompanies him back to his home in Pietrelcina. Once there, Pio is once again able to celebrate Holy Mass the next day as if nothing had happened. But one result of those five weeks spent in the friary at Venafro is that we know without doubt that Padre Pio was offering himself as a victim for the sake of unworthy priests, sinners and souls in Purgatory.

All this time spent away from a friary of the Order he so loved, Pio later spoke of as his time of 'exile'. It pained him to be away from community life. He also suffered increased diabolical attacks, so that he would later refer to the time as his 'double exile', meaning he was separated from his brethren in the religious order and also that he longed for Heaven but was not allowed it.

Tests

Once during this time, Fr Agostino decided to test Pio's intimacy with his Guardian Angel. In September 1912 Agostino wrote him a letter entirely in Greek. Pio brought the letter along to his friend and parish priest at Pietrelcina. Before Don Pannullo could begin to translate it, Pio proceeded to tell him its meaning, word for word.

Later Don Pannullo wrote a testimony at the bottom of that letter. "I, the undersigned, testify on oath that when Padre Pio received this letter he explained its contents to me literally. When I asked him how he could read and explain it as he did not know even the Greek alphabet, he replied: 'You know! My Guardian Angel explained it all to me.' Signed, The Archpriest, Salvatore Pannullo."

At times Fr Agostino also wrote Pio letters in

French and once Padre Pio sent him a reply entirely in French. He explained that his Guardian Angel had told him what to write.

Years later, there are reports of people having confessed to him at San Giovanni Rotondo in different languages and Pio replying to them in their own tongue. This certainly happened to some American and English servicemen who visited him during the Second World War as the Allied Forces were making their way up from southern Italy to re-take Rome from the Germans.

All this time spent away from the friary was certainly unusual for a professed religious. In late 1914 all the details of the 'Padre Pio case' were told to the Superior-General of the Order when he made a visit to the Foggia Province. Fr General said that it was obviously God's will that Pio live outside the community and that he himself would seek the necessary dispensation. On 1st March the following year, 1915, word was received that Pope Benedict XV had granted to Padre Pio "the faculty requested to remain outside the cloister as long as necessary while continuing to wear the habit of his Order".

Spiritual Children

During this time also, both Fr Agostino and Fr Benedetto would recommend particular people to Padre Pio's prayers. Eventually Agostino put one such spiritual child, Raffaelina Cerase, in direct contact with Padre Pio and from March

1914 a correspondence grew up between them. Since his
death this correspondence has been published as one
volume of the existing letters of Padre Pio. The Vice-
Postulator of the Padre's Cause for Canonisation, Fr
Gerardo Di Flumeri, says these letters between Pio and
Raffaelina "are a proof of the Padre's cultural grounding
and that he is not an improvised spiritual director, but an
enlightened guide of souls, sustained by an enviable
theological, ascetic-mystical and biblical training."

With this and numerous other 'spiritual children' in the
coming years, Padre Pio would engage in a prodigious
correspondence. Up until 1922, that is, when all that
would come to a sudden halt!

CONSCRIPTED

The First World War broke out in 1914 and on 23rd May 1915 Italy entered that war. Many of the Capuchin friars were among the men mobilised. Pio himself was soon called up, ordered to present himself to the military office in Benevento on 6th November 1915. In view of his poor health, he was sent from there to Caserta 'for observation' and then to Naples. After one examination in Naples, Pio wrote to Fr Agostino, "I don't know if I will survive this harsh trial. I am unable to stay on my feet, my stomach, as usual, is becoming more and more obstinate and cannot retain any food at all ... The only food I can retain is the Sacred Species.

On 16th December a group of doctors examined him and, diagnosing 'infection of the lungs' they gave him a year's leave for convalescence. He would have to report back for military service in December 1916.

Meanwhile, he returned home to Pietrelcina. Fathers Benedetto and Agostino were now convinced it was time for Pio to return to life in a friary, Agostino telling him in a letter of January 1916 that many people are praying for this intention and also that he believes that in Pio's eventual return to a friary, "the glory of God and the salvation of souls is involved."

By now, the people of Pietrelcina and its surrounds

Private Forgione in military uniform.

were extremely attached to the young extremely pastoral and holy priest living among them. When Fr Agostino visited Pio at home earlier in 1915, word got out among the locals that he had come to take away their very own 'saint'! There was a threat of mob violence and Agostino was told they would have his head off rather then allow him to take away their saint. Don Pannullo had to intervene to restore calm and assure the people that Fr Agostino was not there to take away their Padre Pio!

On subsequent occasions, at San Giovanni Rotondo, the local people also rose up to prevent 'their' Padre Pio being transferred to another friary!

At the end of January 1916 Fr Agostino summons Padre Pio to Foggia, to visit Raffaelina Cerase, who was dying of cancer. Mindful of his experience on his last visit to Pietrelcina, Agostino decided not to go there but to meet Pio on 17th February at Benevento railway station instead! They travelled together from there to Foggia.

A return to community life

The next day, after two years of intense spiritual correspondence, Padre Pio and Raffaelina met for the first time. Agostino describes it as "a reunion between two souls who had known each other for a long time". We do not know what passed between the spiritual father and spiritual child at that first meeting. We do know that the next morning Padre Pio handed over his return ticket to

Pietrelcina to Fr Agostino and wrote home to his mother to send on the rest of his belongings.

For the next few weeks, while residing in the friary at Foggia, Padre Pio visited Raffaelina regularly, until she died on 25th March 1916. What Pio had not known when he came to visit Raffaelina was that she had already offered her life and her suffering as a victim that Padre Pio might be able to return to community life, as Agostino put it, "for the glory of God and the good of souls".

The Capuchins, too, were delighted that their confrere was back among them. One of the friars at Foggia, Fr Alessandro Da Ripabottoni who would later write a book about his dealings with Padre Pio, described him as the life and soul of the community, "a happy spirit, a normal and balanced personality ... never happier than when he was telling humorous stories for the amusement of others."

While they loved having him among them and enjoyed his company, the poor friars at Foggia had also to learn to cope with the diabolical attacks suffered by Padre Pio. While he was the life and soul of the community during the day, at night-time they would hear the infernal racket coming from Pio's cell and would find him so drenched in sweat that he required a complete change of clothes. Under obedience to the Superior, Padre Pio explained that Satan came to his cell at night and the ghastly noises were of the resultant battle which took place between them.

The local bishop came to witness this for himself one

night. For the sake of the brethren in the community, the Superior ordered Padre Pio to pray Christ not to allow these diabolical appearances. The prayer was answered and there were no further night-time disturbances while Pio stayed in that friary.

By day, Padre Pio was overwhelmed by people coming to see him and seek his spiritual counsel. He wrote to Fr Agostino: "I am not left free for a moment; crowds of people thirsting for Jesus are pressing upon me, so that I am at my wits' end."

Poor Padre Pio! This was only but the slightest foretaste of what lay ahead!

San Giovanni

As we have noted, men of fighting age had been mobilised and so the Capuchin province was severely depleted during the years of the First World War. On 4th September 1916 Fr Benedetto assigns Padre Pio to the remote friary further up the mountainside from San Giovanni Rotondo. Pio had asked Benedetto if he could be posted there "where Jesus assures me I will feel better." Still officially an enlisted soldier, Padre Pio duly reported back to the military office in Naples on 18th December 1916. On 30th December he was given leave of absence for another six months and told that he would be notified with a date to report for duty.

Back at San Giovanni Rotondo again, the people soon

began to appreciate the saintly priest. Numbers making the trek up the two kilometre-long mule track from the small town to the friary for morning Mass began to increase. Soon a group would meet with him every week as part of the Franciscan Third Order. They became, in effect, Padre Pio's first prayer group: they would pray together in the friary parlour and he would teach them on some aspect of the spiritual life.

By July 1917, Padre Pio was surprised that he still had not been called back to military service. In fact, there had been a terrible mix-up. The people of San Giovanni Rotondo, of course, knew him only as Padre Pio of Pietrelcina. The telegram which had arrived addressed to Private Francesco Forgione had been returned to the Tenth Medical Corps in Naples, 'addressee unknown'.

Padre Pio the 'deserter'

Local police were then dispatched to Padre Pio's home at Pietrelcina to find 'the deserter'. There, Pio's sister Felicita was able to tell them that Private Forgione was commonly known as Padre Pio and lived in San Giovanni Rotondo. A local police sergeant from that area then turned up at the friary to inform Padre Pio. Unaware of all the fuss over the supposed missing soldier, Pio offered to go there and then with the sergeant. He was assured that that would not be necessary and he duly reported back for duty in Naples the following day.

This time his medical examination showed "infiltration of the pulmonary apexes" but he was still declared "fit for internal service" and was assigned duties as an orderly - or general cleaner and dogsbody. Within a month, his health had broken down again and he was coughing up blood. On 7th October he was admitted to the military hospital in Naples. He continued to suffer fevers with extraordinarily high temperatures. While he and his Capuchin confreres were used to this, medical and nursing staff at the hospital were amazed that his temperature nearly always reached 48 degrees centigrade or more. Pio joked with one nurse that he had better go and fetch a bath thermometer if he did not want another ordinary one broken!

A month later, on 6th November 1917, he was given another four months' sick leave. He duly reported back for duty on 5th March 1918 and on 16th March Private Forgione was, according to his service file, "permanently discharged from the army with good conduct reports". His experiences, though, would leave an impression on him in more ways than one. During the Second World War, he had a great affection for the many American and British servicemen who visited him in San Giovanni Rotondo.

His experience of being a patient in the military hospital was also not wasted, as we shall see.

With four of the younger priests and brothers called up to the military, at the friary of San Giovanni Rotondo, there were only Padre Pio and two other brethren. Pio was kept busy as the numbers climbing the hill from the town below steadily increased. He offered Holy Mass and heard Confessions. He continued to meet and direct his group of lay Franciscans of the Third Order. The depleted community faithfully continued to recite the Prayer of the Church, the Divine Office. From his arrival at San Giovanni Rotondo, Padre Pio had become the spiritual director of the boys' school attached to the friary, the seraphic college. He would hold this post until 1932. The boys were very fond of him and while many of them went on to enter the Capuchins, even those who did not remained in touch with their beloved 'Spiritual Father', coming back to visit him over the years.

Transverberation

It is also remarkable that from his arrival at the friary of San Giovanni Rotondo, every member of that community chose Pio as their spiritual father. When they spoke to him, they did not address him as 'Padre Pio' but as 'Padre Spirituale', Spiritual Father.

It was while carrying out his ministry to the boys of the seraphic college that the Padre was visited by that "celestial person" on the evening of 5th August 1918; that his heart was pierced with a lance.

It is a phenomenon which has been experienced by other great saints of the Church, including the reformer of the Carmelite Order and Doctor of the Church St Teresa of Avila. It is known as 'Transverberation' and marks a point where the saint's heart is somehow seared through with the Word of God, a union of soul with its Redeemer. Her collaborator, the great mystic and also a Doctor of the Church, St John of the Cross, wrote in his treatise 'The Flame of Love': "It can happen that the soul inflamed with the love of God ... will feel overpowered by a Seraphim with a dart or arrow of fiery love..." The saint then remarks that this wound can actually be external and physical and not only symbolic or spiritual. "If God sometimes allows it to appear to the external senses, there will appear a mark that corresponds to the internal wound."

As Padre Pio was a member of a religious order, the Capuchin branch of the Franciscans, he was also bound by a vow of obedience. Throughout his life he lived this vow faithfully. Thus it is that we have an account in the Padre's own words of what took place in August 1918. He is writing under obedience to his Spiritual Director, Fr Benedetto of San Marco in Lamis.

"While I was hearing the boys' confessions on the evening of the 5th, I was suddenly terrorized by the sight of a celestial person who presented himself to my mind's eye. He had in his hand a sort of weapon like a very long sharp-pointed steel blade which seemed to emit fire. At the very instant I saw all this, I saw that person hurl the weapon into my soul with all his might. I cried out with difficulty and felt I was dying. I asked the boys to leave because I felt ill and no longer able to continue.

"The agony lasted uninterruptedly until the morning of the 7th. I cannot tell you how much I suffered during this period of anguish. Even my entrails were torn and ruptured by the weapon, and nothing was spared. From that day on I have been mortally wounded."

Reading this, one might think that the 31 year-old priest was exaggerating, or at least speaking metaphorically to describe some interior spiritual experience. He wasn't!

He truly was wounded with an opening in his side into his heart that would bleed for the rest of his life, another fifty years. A month to the day of his heart being thus pierced, he wrote, "The wound which has been reopened bleeds incessantly. This alone is enough to make me die a thousand times."

For three days after it happened he remained in bed, bleeding, hoping to hide what had happened to him. From then on throughout the rest of his life, he would dress this wound with a handkerchief, having to change the bloodied cloth several times throughout the day.

Padre Pio was greatly embarrassed at being singled out like this. He also feared that he may have offended the Lord in some way and was being punished. Pio's confessor, Father Agostino (who would later become Guardian of the Friary of San Giovanni Rotondo) tried to reassure him in a letter of 24th August 1918. He pointed out to him that the Transverberation had taken place on the vigil of the Feast of Christ's Transfiguration when God the Father cried out,

"Behold, this is my beloved Son, in whom I am well pleased." (cf Matthew 17:5) and that far from being a punishment, was "a further proof of His (God's) love".

Father Benedetto wrote, "Yours is not a purgation but a painful union. The fact of the wound completes your passion just as it completed the Passion of the Beloved on the Cross."

Ever-obedient, Padre Pio came to understand that just as Our Lord poured out his life for us, even unto death on the Cross and the piercing of his heart, so he too, a priest of Christ and His Church, would pour his own life out for love of God and His people. It happened after Pio had finally been dispensed from any other requirement as to military service and had thus begun his 'definitive' stay at San Giovanni Rotondo. And it took place while he was administering the Mercy of God in the Sacrament of Confession.

PADRE PIO THE CONFESSOR

For the first years of his priesthood Padre Pio had been unable to hear confessions. He had completed his studies privately at home (while under the guidance of his superiors and with the aid of Don Pannullo, nevertheless). But because he was not present with his fellows at the final courses before ordination, he was not automatically granted a faculty to hear Confessions. During what he later called his 'years of exile', when he was forced to live at home in Pietrelcina, he once wrote to his superiors requesting that he be licensed to hear confessions in order to help out Don Pannullo in Holy Week. The reply from Fr Benedetto was that they were afraid that hearing confessions would put a further strain on his health and make him even more ill than he already was.

His spiritual daughter, Raffaelina Cerase, who offered her final illness and her life for a return of Pio to community life and public ministry, had prophesied to Fr Agostino that Pio would save many souls through that sacrament. Today many refer to him as the 'martyr of the confessional'.

We have read that in 1910 and in 1911 Pio's stigmata had been for short times visible. His prayers, along with those of his friend Don Pannullo, had been answered and the Lord took away the visible signs. Now the plan of God seemed to have different designs.

Still suffering from the piercing of his heart, but no longer confined to bed, Pio was back into his routine of carrying out his duties and celebrating Mass and the Divine Office. On Friday morning the 20th September 1918, he offered Mass in the friary church of Our Lady of Grace, probably at the side altar of St Francis. After Mass, as was his custom, he retired to the friars' tribune situated on an upper-level balcony at the back of the church, in order to continue his prayer and make his thanksgiving.

There were (and still are) three tiered rows of pews. Usually Pio sat in the second one, but this day he sat in the front seat. Directly in front of him was a large crucifix attached to the front of the tribune.

As he wrote an account of events a month later, under obedience to Father Benedetto, we have Padre Pio's own words as to what occurred in the tribune of the church of Our Lady of Grace that Friday morning.

Stigmata

"What can I tell you regarding my crucifixion? My God! What embarrassment and humiliation I suffer by being obliged to explain what you have done to this wretched creature!

"On the morning of the 20th of last month, in the choir, after I had celebrated Mass I yielded to a drowsiness similar to a sweet sleep. All the internal and external senses and even the very faculties of my soul

Under obedience to his superiors, Padre Pio allowed this photo to be taken of his stigmata.

were immersed in indescribable stillness. Absolute silence surrounded and invaded me. I was suddenly filled with great peace and abandonment which effaced everything else and caused a lull in the turmoil. All this happened in a flash.

"While this was taking place I saw before me a mysterious person similar to the one I had seen on the evening of 5th August. The only difference was that his hands and feet and side were dripping blood. This sight terrified me and what I felt at that moment is indescribable. I thought I should die and really should have died if the Lord had not intervened and strengthened my heart which was about to burst out of my chest.

The vision disappeared and I became aware that my hands, feet and side were dripping blood." (Letters, Vol 1, 22nd October 1918)

Somehow, he dragged himself back to his cell. He bound up his wounds as best he could and for the next day or two tried his best to keep his hands hidden beneath the long sleeves of his habit. He was suffering both physically and spiritually. In a letter to Fr Benedetto on 22nd October 1918, he wrote: "Dear Father, I am dying of pain because of the wounds and the resulting embarrassment I feel deep in my soul. I am afraid I shall bleed to death if the Lord does not hear my heartfelt supplication to relieve me of this condition."

On this occasion, the Lord did not see fit to answer

Pio's prayer. The wounds were there to stay and Padre Pio would bleed from them every day and night for the next 50 years. He would be the only priest in the history of the Church to be recognised as bearing the stigmata of the wounds of Christ.

His own patron, the patron of Italy and founder of his religious family, St Francis of Assisi, bore the stigmata. Francis was not a priest but a deacon. And the stigmata were given to him only in the last two years of his life, thought to be a gift for him personally. With Padre Pio, it seems, they were to be a public sign, a gift not only for him but for the good of the whole Church and the world; a charism.

Despite Pio's initial attempt, in his embarrassment and confusion, to keep the wounds hidden, Fr Guardian of the friary soon recognised something was amiss. On the second or third day after the 20th September, he came to Padre Pio's cell to confront him. Poor Pio burst into tears and 'admitted' everything to his superior as he told him all that had happened.

Padre Pio under siege

As best they could, everyone made efforts to keep the news within the confines of the friary and the Order. Inevitably, though, within a few months, word began to spread and crowds began to flock to the friary of Our Lady of Grace at San Giovanni Rotondo. Soon, Padre Pio was under siege, a state he would live in for the rest of his

life as people came from near and far; to assist at his
Holy Mass, to confess to him, to touch him, just to catch
a glimpse of the holy friar.

Already by June of the following year, 1919, he would
be writing to Fr Benedetto to say he had no more time to
reply to letters as he was hearing confessions constantly.
"I haven't a free moment. All my time is spent in setting
my brothers free from the snares of Satan. ... This is
precisely what I am doing by night and by day."

It was at this early stage that the only photographs
taken of Pio deliberately displaying the wounds in his
hands were taken. He was ordered to allow this by his
superiors and a couple of photos exist of the Padre in the
friary garden with his two hands held up, crossed over his
breast. For the rest of the time, he took to wearing
woollen mittens to cover the palms of his hands. Of
course, he had to remove these when offering the
Sacrifice of the Mass and the friars made extra long
sleeves on his alb, lined with red material, in order to
allow him some privacy and not have the wounds the
subject of unseemly gawping. However, at those
moments when the priest had to raise the Sacred Host and
the Chalice, of course his sleeves would often slip a little
and there exist photos of some of those moments when
the bloody wounds could be seen.

In June 1919 the first of the press arrived at San
Giovanni Rotondo. Throughout the rest of his life, Padre

Pio would be the subject of all sorts of weird and wonderful stories invented by the media. Even today, newspapers in Italy will use the image of Padre Pio, or a supposed 'story' regarding him, in order to sell more copies.

Yet the Church teaches that the mass media are a "gift from God" (cf. Encyclical *Miranda Prorsus,* 1957) and thanks to the presence of a BBC film crew there exists film footage of the Padre's last ever Mass, offered hours before his death, in 1968.

During his life, though, false and extravagant claims and stories were sometimes circulated by those wishing to support Padre Pio. Inversely, others made harsh judgements and sometimes false accusations. Throughout all the claims and counter-claims, Pio stuck fast to his sure lifeline; obedience to his legitimate superiors.

Obedience

As San Giovanni Rotondo became a town under siege, and the friary struggled to cope with the throngs of visitors seeking access to their church, some clergy of the local diocese were not best pleased. Complaints and accusations were made to Rome. On two particular occasions Padre Pio would be placed under certain restrictions by the Holy Office.

As part of the first such judgement by the Holy Office, in June 1922, it was suggested that Padre Pio be moved from San Giovanni Rotondo. The local people rose up. They signed petitions en masse requesting that their beloved Padre Pio be allowed to stay among them, the first of these being presented to the Father Guardian by the Mayor himself. They petitioned Rome. They sent delegations to the local Archbishop and even to the Vatican itself. In 1922, and again at other moments during the 1920s and 1930s when there was word of transferring Padre Pio, the townspeople organised a 24-hour guard around the friary to ensure that the authorities could not spirit the Padre away, through some side entrance or during the night.

The Mayor told one bishop that it was not the fact that Pio might be moved that the people objected to, but that he might be moved due to false allegations as if he were guilty of doing something wrong.

In the early years, Padre Pio was sometimes subjected to embarrassing and painful examination of his wounds by doctors, on the instructions of his Order and/or the Vatican. He would do whatever was demanded of him by his religious vow of obedience. His compliance to this in every detail is another sign as to how he lived all his Baptismal and Religious vows to the letter. One instance illustrates how he would do so, whatever the cost to himself.

A visit from Milan

Pio had been ordered not to show his wounds to anyone without written instruction from the Capuchin Generalate in Rome. Once, in April 1920, a distinguished cleric from the north of Italy, who was at once a priest, a medical doctor, a psychologist, a theologian and the founder of a university, arrived at the friary of Our Lady of Grace. He said he had come at the order of the Holy Office to see Padre Pio and demanded to examine his wounds. When he could not produce the required authorisation from the Capuchin headquarters, Padre Pio dismissed him in short measure.

The priest in question (a good friend of the Archbishop of Milan who would later become Pope Pius XI), went on, nevertheless, to write a 'report' on Padre Pio, detailing among other things his supposed (and in fact non-existent) examination of the Padre's wounds. This priest dismissed all stigmatics, apart from St Francis of Assisi, as neurotics and frauds and it is reported that he caused some delay in the beatification process of Saint Gemma Galgani, the young mystic and stigmatic from Lucca who was a lay associate of the Passionists.

To those who would argue that the stigmata were the result of too much meditation on the crucified Jesus, Padre Pio's retort was ; 'Go out to the fields. Look at and meditate upon a bull. See if you grow horns!'

Vatican intervention

The 1920s saw several enquiries by the Vatican and the arrival of 'Apostolic Visitors' to San Giovanni Rotondo. Whenever there were restrictions placed upon him, such as that he should not celebrate Mass in public, or he was banned from hearing confessions for a period, some would venture that Padre Pio should do something to defend himself. To such people Padre Pio gave very short shrift indeed. With a glare that cut them to the quick, he would retort: "Don't you know that you should kiss the hand of your mother, even when it is her hand that disciplines you?" The message was clear: the Church is our Mother. We venerate her whether we understand or like what She is doing or not, in the knowledge that She wills our greatest good.

Padre Pio remained devoted to his own earthly parents too, both of whom spent their last days and died at San Giovanni Rotondo. When Pio had first experienced the visible stigmata briefly in 1910 and 1911, Father Agostino had written him a letter assuring him that they were gifts from the Lord, that he should kiss this sign of the Lord's love for him. Ever-obedient, Padre Pio for the rest of his life would kiss the wounds in his hands when he vested for Mass in the same way he would venerate with a kiss the priestly stole he was about to put on.

On visits, Padre Pio's father Grazio would often make to kiss his son's wounded hand. Pio would pull his hand away, saying, "No, no. It is for the son to kiss his father's hand." Once, though, Grazio was too quick for his son, and managed to grab Pio's hand and kiss it. Afterwards, the glint in his eye showed satisfaction as if to say, 'There, did it!'

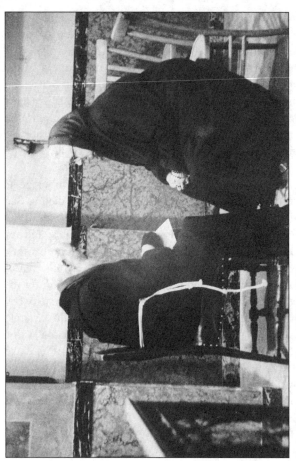

Padre Pio in conversation with Mary Pyle.

'L'Americana'

As to this day, the crowds pouring to San Giovanni
Rotondo did not diminish, but only increased. In 1923 a
young American lady, Mary Pyle, the daughter of a
wealthy Protestant family, who had become a Catholic
in 1918, arrived in Italy. She worked with the famous
Italian Doctor Maria Montessori as her interpreter on
her travels and came with a friend to see the renowned
stigmatist. She confessed to Padre Pio. Afterwards, she
told friends, she could not get the impression of "a saint
living in this world" out of her mind. She returned to
San Giovanni Rotondo, this time along with Maria
Montessori, in 1924, and told the Padre she wanted to
live near him. From her own patrimony, Mary built a
villa slightly down the hill from the friary. In 1925
Padre Pio himself enrolled her as a member into the
Third Order of Franciscans. A close spiritual bond
continued between Padre Pio and the lady the locals
affectionately called 'l'Americana'. Until her death a
few months before the Padre's in 1968, she acted in a
sense as Padre Pio's hostess outside the friary. She
accommodated pilgrims, answered their questions, and
helped the people of different nationality and language
who began to arrive. It was in Mary's house that
Giuseppa Forgione died on 3rd January 1929, and
Grazio Forgione died there on the Feast of the Holy
Rosary, 7th October, 1946.

Restrictions

On 11th June 1931, the Father Guardian of the friary had the sad task of communicating to Padre Pio news of the latest set of restrictions to be laid upon him by the Holy Office. He may not celebrate Holy Mass in public. He may not hear Confessions, either of the faithful or of his religious confreres (and remember, every one of the community chose Pio as his spiritual father).

Father Guardian noted that he told all this to Padre Pio after vespers. Pio's response: "And he, lifting his eyes to Heaven, said: 'May the will of God be done!' Then he covered his eyes with his hands, bowed his head and didn't breathe another word."

From the next day, until the order was rescinded two years later, Padre Pio celebrated Holy Mass in the friary's internal chapel. His Mass would take anything from one and a half to three hours. He would spend hours in private prayer and, as he was no longer allowed to hear confessions, which had taken up most of his daytime hours until then, he spent hour after hour in the friary library. It is suggested that in the two years of his isolation he probably read every theological and spiritual book in the library at least once. Although he barely ate, he was commanded to attend the midday meal in refectory and out of obedience tried his best to nibble at a piece of food.

The Seraphic College, to which Padre Pio had been the devoted spiritual director since his arrival in San

Giovanni Rotondo, was closed down in 1932 and transferred to another friary.

During this time that Padre referred to later as his 'imprisonment', the people continued to come to San Giovanni Rotondo. Busloads of pilgrims would arrive and pray the Rosary outside the friary for a return of Padre Pio to public ministry, particularly that of confessor. The people's spiritual need must have pained him. Back in 1919, in the first year after his stigmatisation, he had written to Fr Agostino: "Ask Fr Provincial to send many workers into the Lord's vineyard because it is real cruelty and tyranny to send away hundreds and even thousands of people a day when they come from far away for the sole purpose of being cleansed from their sins and are unable to do so for lack of confessors." (Letters Vol 1, 14th June 1919)

Two years after this 'imprisonment' began, the newly-appointed archbishop of the area made his first visit to the parish of San Giovanni Rotondo, on 23rd June 1932. The people turned out en masse to beg the archbishop's intercession for the liberation of their Padre Pio.

Back to work

Three weeks later, on 15th July 1932, the Father Provincial arrived at San Giovanni Rotondo, having just been to Rome. At the midday meal in the refectory, he made an announcement: Padre Pio may henceforth celebrate Holy

Mass in public and he may hear the confessions of priests and religious brothers within the cloister. Pio stood up and went over to where Fr Provincial was sitting. He went down on his knees and asked Fr to thank His Holiness the Pope for his paternal goodness.

Fr Guardian of the friary told Pio to go to the window and greet the crowds. They applauded enthusiastically at the first sign of their beloved Padre in two years. Then the community took Padre Pio down to open the friary doors and bless the cheering crowds who thronged around him.

The next day, the Feast of Our Lady of Mount Carmel, 16th July 1932, Padre Pio once more offered the Holy Sacrifice of the Mass in the public church. Fr Guardian reported the "visible and profound" emotion of those present and a "truly edifying silence" in the packed church.

From 25th March 1934 Pio was once more allowed to hear the men's confessions. In the following days, the friary annals record that Padre Pio and the other friars were in the confessional from dawn until mid-day, because "the influx of men was enormous. From 12th May he was allowed to resume hearing the women's confessions and the friary annals record that he was now hearing an average of 60 confessions a day and, "during feast days, much more."

Home for the Relief of Suffering

Padre Pio was concerned not only with the interior or spiritual well-being of the faithful. Already in 1925 he had founded the Civil Hospital of St Francis, situated in a former Poor Clare convent in the town of San Giovanni Rotondo. It had two seven-bed wards, two smaller rooms and an operating theatre.

It was soon apparent that this was not sufficient and Padre Pio had the grandiose dream of a massive hospital complex right there next to the friary on the mountainside. It would be another two decades from 1925, however, before work would even begin on that.

In 1938 the Civil Hospital of St Francis was severely damaged in an earthquake. It was later restored as a kindergarten but, once again, San Giovanni Rotondo was without a hospital. On 9th January 1940 a small committee was formed "for the foundation of a clinic in accordance with Padre Pio's intentions." At their first meeting, "It is agreed that everything undertaken must be subject to Padre Pio's advice."

That same evening, the men of the committee were admitted to the friary to meet with the Padre. Although he himself refused to be on the committee, in the coming years he would meet regularly of an evening with those involved in building the hospital. At that first such meeting, he rummaged in the pocket of his habit and produced a gold coin, given to him as a donation for his charitable work. "Here," he said, "I want to be the first to make an offering for the Home for the Relief of Suffering".

In that way also was announced the name of the new project. In Padre Pio's mind it was not just to be a hospital for the treatment of sickness or disease. It was to be a place where people felt at home, where the whole person was taken care of. And Pio was clear as to the principles of its construction: it must be large, airy and light, and only the best materials were to be used; nothing was too good for the sick.

Money began to pour in from the Padre's spiritual children around the world. Former ex-servicemen who had visited San Giovanni Rotondo, Italian ex-patriots in the United States, all sorts of people contributed to the funds. An English woman, Barbara Ward, at the time assistant editor of The Economist magazine, was instrumental in obtaining the grant of a large sum in 1948.

Construction work had already begun by then, when Padre Pio was invited to push the button to detonate the first explosion of rock from the mountainside opposite the friary on 19th May 1947. It was a massive project and would become the largest and finest hospital in the whole of the south of Italy.

A new Church in Pietrelcina

In 1951 a new Capuchin friary and church, largely financed by Mary Pyle, were inaugurated in Padre Pio's home town of Pietrelcina. There had been the thought of bringing the Padre there to assist at the ceremonies. Mindful of the local uprisings on previous occasions when there was threat of moving Padre Pio, the authorities were fearful! Padre Pio, it seems, was present though, through bilocation. When he was asked whether he would attend the opening ceremonies, Pio calmly replied, "I will be present in Pietrelcina and at the same time I'll be in the Confessional at San Giovanni Rotondo."

When the Fr Guardian of the new friary visited San Giovanni Rotondo a few days after the inauguration he expressed the hope that Padre Pio would some day visit it. Pio replied that he knew it better even than the new Fr Guardian and went on to describe it in the utmost detail, even to the number of steps on the stairway in the entrance. The Fr Guardian, Padre Alberto, wrote, "In fact, I didn't know how many steps there were, because I had never counted them. I think Padre Pio was in the friary church in Pietrelcina by bilocation."

Work continued on the Home for the Relief of Suffering. A nursing school was set up to train staff. The friary of Our Lady of Grace would supply the chaplaincy. (While in the beginning, there was one chaplain, today there are half a dozen. They live in the

Home, offer Mass in the Home's own chapel, and only return to the friary on their days off.)

The Hospital opens

In July 1954 the outpatients department began functioning and in November of the same year the blood bank became operational. Finally, nearly sixteen years after Padre Pio had made that first monetary donation towards the construction, the Home for the Relief of Suffering was opened on the Padre's Name Day, 5th May, 1956.

The honours were done jointly by Padre Pio and by Bologna's Cardinal Lercaro. The Cardinal said, "Where there is charity, there is love; where there is love, there is God. ... Have you noticed this in San Giovanni Rotondo? Yes. The whole world has become aware of it. God is here; therefore, love and charity are also here."

When the home opened, it had 300 beds. Soon this was not enough. On the second anniversary of the opening Padre Pio detonated a mine to start the excavation work for a new extension. Another wing was added in 1966, bringing the total number of beds to 600, double the original capacity. Today, that number has doubled again as there are now more than 1200 beds in Padre Pio's Home for the Relief of Suffering.

All this building work was possible in no short measure thanks to the donations that poured in from the Padre's spiritual children the world over. In fact, a whole movement was to grow up, which would become known as 'Padre Pio Prayer Groups'. We have read how Pio had been directing groups of lay people who came together to pray since his stay in Foggia in 1916.

Prayer groups

It was in 1950 that he launched his official appeal to his spiritual children to come together in groups to pray. In the letter of invitation sent out from the friary to his thousands of spiritual children, the guidelines were simple and clear: They were to meet at least once a month, "with no other goal than that of praying and inviting other friends to know prayer." No such group should be formed without the permission of the local bishop, nor function without the direction of a priest appointed by the bishop.

Today there are thousands of such 'Padre Pio Prayer Groups' throughout the world. In 1980 they would fill the 10,000-seater Audience Hall 'lent' to them for a congress by the Vatican. But their first congress would take place in San Giovanni Rotondo in September 1968, to mark the fiftieth anniversary of the stigmata. As it turned out, they would be there for their founder's death and funeral.

A special visit

While Padre Pio must have received hundreds of thousands, if not millions, of visitors and penitents during his fifty years of priestly ministry at San Giovanni

Rotondo, nevertheless Providence allows one to note the presence of the individual extraordinary visitor.

In 1947 a young Polish priest, undertaking post-graduate studies in Rome, made the journey south to San Giovanni Rotondo. He made his confession to the stigmatised friar. In 1974, as Archbishop of Krakow, Karol Wojytla returned as a pilgrim and prayed at the Padre's tomb. As Pope, it was he who gave permission to the Archbishop of Manfredonia to institute the local process towards the friar's eventual beatification. And as Pope, it was he who declared Padre Pio Blessed before hundreds of thousands of the faithful who filled St Peter's Square and the entire length of the Via della Conciliazione and surrounding streets, televisually linked with the crowds gathered outside St John Lateran Basilica and also those gathered at San Giovanni Rotondo.

When the 42 year-old Bishop of Krakow (it was before he was officially installed as Archbishop) arrived in Rome for the opening session of the Second Vatican Council in 1962, he was concerned about a dear friend of his. Before leaving Poland, he had learned that Dr Wanda Poltawska, survivor of the Nazi concentration camps and the mother of four young girls, was suffering from a serious cancer.

On 18th November 1962, Bishop Wojtyla wrote from Rome to Padre Pio, in Latin, stating his fears for Wanda and asking the Padre's prayers. At that time Padre Pio was receiving some 2,000 letters per week. When the priest assisting him read out the letter, Pio said , "Oh, we can't refuse him."

By now Wanda was in hospital and was due to be operated upon on a Friday morning. On the Saturday morning Bishop Wojtyla telephone Poland to her husband Andrzej. The operation had not taken place after all! On a final pre-operative examination, all traces of the tumour had disappeared!

Bishop Wojtyla again wrote, in Latin, to thank Padre Pio for his prayers. Out of the thousands of letters he was then receiving every month, Pio told his priest assistant; "File those letters. Some day they will be important."

When as Pope John Paul II, Wojtyla made a Papal visit to San Giovanni Rotondo (and to the Grotto of St Michael) in 1987, he once again prayed at the Padre's tomb. And there among the honoured guests at the Papal Mass was his old friend Dr Wanda Poltawska.

Owning the hospital

After the opening of the Home for the Relief of Suffering, there arose the question of legal ownership. Padre Pio was clear; he was a Franciscan friar vowed to poverty in all things and a special Chapter of the Capuchins decided that it would go against their spirit of poverty to own such a building. Padre Pio willed the Home to the Holy See. A year after its official opening, Pope Pius XII named Padre Pio as Administrator of the Home for the Relief of Suffering.

The Padre Pio Prayer Groups are attached to the Home for the Relief of Suffering. Padre Pio willed these too to the Holy See. Shortly before the Padre's death, the Vatican confided their co-ordination to the Fr Guardian of the Capuchin community at San Giovanni Rotondo.

Further illness

The 1960s saw Pio's health weakening further. The year 1960 saw the fiftieth anniversary of his ordination to the priesthood. The friars wondered whether he would see the fiftieth anniversary of his stigmatisation. He kept on working. He once said, "I would prefer to be brought to the confessional in a chair rather than not hear confessions anymore." And in his final months he was transported by wheelchair. He was also given permission to celebrate Holy Mass seated.

While the Home was being built, the Capuchins had also to come to terms with the fact that numbers were not going to cease coming to San Giovanni Rotondo: the little friary church simply could not hold them. A new church of Our Lady of Grace was built next to the original one and was opened on 1st July 1959. At a push it can hold perhaps 1,000 people. When Padre Pio saw it, he said simply, "It's too small." At weekends and on holy days, the crowds amass on the giant piazza constructed in front of the two churches.

While the new church was completed, work continued on constructing a confessional chapel. The Order had also planned a final resting place for Padre Pio. His tomb would be prepared under the new church. When he heard this, the Padre told them: "When it's ready, I will die."

On 25th July 1968, Pope Paul VI issued his encyclical letter '*Humanae Vitae*'. In September of that year the Capuchin Order was holding its General Chapter meeting in Rome and would have an audience with the Pope. Pio dictated a letter, dated 12th September 1968, in which he expressed his filial devotion to the Vicar of Christ. Paul VI was under attack from all sides for his encyclical and Padre Pio wrote: "I thank you also, in the name of my spiritual children and 'Prayer Groups' for the clear and decided words you have given us in the recent encyclical *Humanae Vitae*, and I reaffirm my faith, my unconditional obedience to your illuminated instructions."

It was the last letter Padre Pio ever wrote.

Last days

The fiftieth anniversary of Pio's reception of the stigmata would take place on 20th September 1968. His prayer groups were gathering for an international congress, the opening Mass of which would take place on 22nd September.

Mary Pyle had died in April of that year. Many of the Padre's old collaborators in the building of the Home for the Relief of Suffering had gone to their eternal reward. His own health continued to decline and in the latter months the friars were convinced he was preparing to take his leave of them.

Padre Pio would celebrate the opening Mass of the prayer group congress, in thanksgiving for the Holy See's recent recognition of them. He was wheeled in his chair from the friary to the new church to celebrate the 5am Mass. The church was packed to capacity. At the end of Mass, as he had risen from his seat and was leaving the High Altar, Padre Pio almost collapsed. He would have fallen but for the quick action of a young American friar who was one of the Padre's assistants in his last years. Father Joseph Pius caught Pio in his arms and, with the help of another friar, escorted him from the sanctuary. Padre Pio continued to bless the crowds as he was escorted away, repeating, "My children, my children".

He was taken to his cell to rest. At ten o'clock that morning Father Guardian of the friary blessed the now-completed tomb prepared for Padre Pio in the crypt of the new church. At that precise moment, Pio asked to be taken to a window to bless the crowds gathered in the piazza. The crowds went crazy, cheering and waving their handkerchiefs in response to the Padre's greeting. In the evening he had himself wheeled to a balcony in the new church to bless the crowds who had assisted at an evening Mass there. Those who couldn't get into the church had gathered in a field below the friary. Back in his cell, from his window he blessed these crowds. Just then, a fellow priest of the community, Fr Raffale looked in to see how he was. Pio said, "I belong more to the other world than to this one. Pray that I might die."

Padre Pio's death

That night, surrounded by all his brethren of the friary and his doctor, Padre Pio gave up his spirit at 2.30am. The wounds in his hands, feet and side had all healed over, and Fr Guardian ordered these to be photographed for the historical record. As Father Joseph Pius put it, "His ministry was finished, so the signs were finished."

The next day Padre Pio's mortal remains, in a glass-topped coffin, were placed before the altar in the new church. The church had to remain open night and day to allow as many as possible of those who wished to venerate his remains to pass before the coffin. At midday on the 26th September the funeral rites began. The coffin was taken in procession through the throngs of more than 100,000 people who packed the streets of San Giovanni Rotondo. Back at the church, the Requiem Mass began at 7pm. At 10pm Padre Pio's mortal remains were laid to rest in the recently-completed tomb in the crypt. The next day the stream of pilgrims coming to pray at his tomb began. It has not stopped since.

A new and bigger church has been built slightly down the mountainside from the friary. It was opened on the 1st July 2004 and holds 10,000 people. One wall opens up onto a piazza which can accommodate 30,000 more.

Witnesses of a holy death

Padre Pio's death was clearly a holy event which marked hundreds of thousands of people around the world. One woman who lived it in a remarkable way was Padre Pio's first spiritual child, the one entrusted to him directly by Our Lady the day the girl was born in 1905; Giovanna Rizzani. She had come to San Giovanni Rotondo at the time of the prayer group congress and confessed to Padre Pio on 19th September 1968. He told her, "This is the last confession you will have with me." When she asked why, he replied, "Because I am leaving. My hour has arrived. Jesus is coming to meet me."

A day or two after all the commotion of Padre Pio's funeral, Giovanna spoke to one of the Capuchin friars, Fr Alberto. She recounted how, on the night of his death, while she was in the bedroom of the boarding house where she had found accommodation, she somehow 'witnessed' Padre Pio's death. To the astonishment of Fr Alberto, she said, "OK, let me describe to you what I saw and you can just answer yes or no, true or false." Giovanna then described every detail; who was present, including such detail as the friar who was holding a clean habit over his arm to clothe the Padre in after death. She described in minute detail the form and content of Padre

Pio's cell, which at that time had never been photographed; the first photo of the cell, left as it was when Pio died, was taken in December 1969.

A Holy Priest

What was the meaning of the life and death of Padre Pio of Pietrelcina, to whose tomb literally millions of people make pilgrimage every year?

In his homily at the Mass of Beatification in St Peter's Square, on Sunday 2nd May 1999, Pope John Paul said, "The face of Padre Pio reflected the light of the Resurrection. His body, marked by the 'stigmata', showed forth the intimate bond between death and resurrection which characterizes the Paschal Mystery. Blessed Pio of Pietrelcina shared in the Passion with a special intensity: the unique gifts which were given to him, and the interior and mystical sufferings which accompanied them, allowed him constantly to participate in the Lord's agonies, never wavering in his sense that 'Calvary is the hill of the saints'."

And in a homily the next day, John Paul quoted his predecessor: "The description of Pope Paul VI of the Servant of God is most apt: 'See what fame Padre Pio had! But why? Because he said Mass humbly, he confessed from morning to evening, and he was a representative stamped with the stigmata of Our Lord. He was a man of prayer and suffering.' (Paul VI, 20th February 1971)"

To another spiritual daughter, who was cured of cancer through the Padre's prayers, the message of his life is quite clear. Dr Wanda Poltawska says, "His long hours in the confessional are an example to priests who have lost their belief in the Sacrament of Penance and proclaim general absolution. The way he celebrated Holy Mass is a sign for those who say the Mass quickly and without adoration.

"We all need to learn from his obedience and humility in accepting even unjust orders from the Church. Padre Pio, whose everyday life was so penetrated by the supernatural, is a saint for modern man, oppressed by materialism, devoid of spiritual life."

Saint Padre Pio, pray for holy priests. Saint Pio of Pietrelcina, pray for us.

The statue in Piazza degli Olmi by Pericle Fazzini.

THE SHRINE

San Giovanni Rotondo

To get to San Giovanni Rotondo is not easy!

Most people travelling from Britain and other English-speaking countries would probably go as part of an organised group. This is to be recommended!

For those travelling independently, Sita buses leave from the square outside the railway station of Foggia. Buses leave approximately once an hour on weekdays (reduced service on Sundays and holidays) and you need to buy your bus ticket inside the railway station first!

Although San Giovanni Rotondo is only eighteen miles from Foggia, don't expect a quick half-hour journey! After a few miles of highway, once the bus starts ascending the mountain, the road twists and gets steeper the further you go.

To arrive at the Shrine, remain on the bus as it travels first through the town of San Giovanni Rotondo. The Capuchin friary and Shrine of Our Lady of Grace is situated further up the mountain from the town of San Giovanni Rotondo itself.

Passing through a square in the town (Piazza degli Olmi), you will see a bronze statue of Padre Pio. It was the last work produced by the sculptor Pericle Fazzini. The poet Ungaretti described him as "the sculptor of wind". The statue of the Padre himself shows him elevating a monstrance, summarizing his whole priestly ministry of revealing Jesus to the people. This portion of the sculpture stands on a lower section portraying four episodes of Padre's life: in one he is threatening with a pitchfork a friend who tried to persuade the Padre as a youngster not to devote his life to Our Lord; another episode portrays the devil tempting Padre Pio; a third shows him administering the Sacrament of Confession; in the final one he is seen receiving the stigmata, the marks of Christ's Passion.

The town of San Giovanni Rotondo is said to take its name from the fact that when it was founded as a Roman settlement there was a circular temple there dedicated to the god Janus. With the arrival of Christianity the residents demolished the temple and built a church dedicated to St John the Baptist. When Padre Pio arrived there in 1916, the town itself was circular in shape. It was poor and isolated, with no running water, no sewage system, no electricity. Being 1800 feet above sea level in the Gargano Mountains, it was relatively late before proper roads were constructed and one could reach it by motorised transport. The first time Padre Pio travelled to the place it was on the back of a horse-drawn cart. He wrote that days later, he still felt his bones shuddering! After his discharge from military service in 1918, Pio attended a meeting of Capuchins in San Marco la Catola. Travelling back by modern motor car with some of his confreres, there was a mishap. The car broke down. The Padre later wrote in a letter: "The effect of the breakdown itself and of having to spend the whole night out there in the open country upset my nervous system so much I am just beginning to get over it."

The small Capuchin friary at San Giovanni Rotondo had been founded at the request of the local people, who paid for it to be built between 1538 and 1540 on land donated by a local benefactor. After an earthquake in 1624 it had to be rebuilt and a church dedicated to Our Lady of Grace was built in 1676. Above the door there is a charming lunette depicting the Madonna and Child, along with St Francis of Assisi and St Michael the Archangel. On either side of the doorway one can find two plaques, both placed by the Municipality of San Giovanni Rotondo; one in 1960 marking Padre Pio's priestly golden jubilee, the other in 1968 marking the fiftieth anniversary of his stigmatisation. Inside the church one can see the altar of St Francis where Padre Pio so often celebrated Holy Mass.

The old church opens at 5.30am and closes at 6.30pm. Mass is offered here by priests leading groups of pilgrims, starting at 6.30am.

The new church, consecrated in 1959, was built adjoining the old church and there is an interconnecting doorway. It has a nave and two side aisles. At the far end of the nave, on the wall of the apse, there is a giant mosaic depicting Our Lady of Grace. It was designed by

Professor Bedini and produced by the Vatican School of Mosaic. The magnificent mosaics on the side altars on either side of the church were likewise manufactured by the Vatican School of Mosaic.

The painting of Our Lady of Grace was crowned by Cardinal Tedeschini on 2nd July 1959, the day after the new church was consecrated. For this reason, the new church is commonly referred to as the shrine. It is open from 5.30am to 7.15pm. There is normally a Holy Mass offered every hour from 8am to noon, and one at 5.30pm. Again, because of the large number of pilgrim groups visiting San Giovanni Rotondo, one can often find Holy Mass being celebrated for them by their own chaplains at other times. On weekdays, the Evening Prayer of the Church is said in the Shrine at 6.30pm. At particular holiday periods, such as Christmas, Easter, the Assumption of Our Lady, the Feast of All Saints, as well as anniversaries connected to Padre Pio - his ordination, his stigmatisation, his death - be warned: the crowds are enormous. Events usually start the evening before and include an all-night vigil. Because of the enormity of the crowds, all this takes place outside on the piazza, though with the completion of the new church complex these will no doubt take place there.

To the right of the shrine, there is a door which leads down stairs to a confessional chapel, where confessions are heard in many languages. Access is also gained to

Padre Pio's tomb, where people come to pray from morning to night. There is also an altar there and some groups, by special arrangement with the friars, may have Holy Mass there.

Standing facing the old church and the shrine from the huge piazza built in front of them (and where Holy Mass is celebrated at weekends and holy days) turn right and look up. The flags of all the world fluttering there are atop the largest hospital in southern Italy, the Home for the Relief of Suffering, founded by Padre Pio. On weekday afternoons there is usually the opportunity to join a guided visit.

As you once again face the old church and the shrine, to your left, graduating down the hillside, is the 'new' new church, opened in autumn 2002. Designed by architect Renzo Piano, it seats some 10,000 people. One wall opens out onto a piazza to accommodate larger crowds on weekends and holy days. Incorporated into the new church complex is a large confessional chapel. There are also pilgrim facilities, such as conference halls, refectory and toilets. The lower, crypt level houses exhibitions outlining the Padre's life, displaying relics, and also linking right through to the Padre's tomb underneath the shrine.

Back on the piazza of the old church and the shrine, this time facing down the road leading to the town, a couple of hundred yards down, on your right-hand side, is a pink villa; the house built by Mary Pyle.

Once again facing the old church and the shrine, looking again to your right, on the other side of the public road leading to the Home for the Relief of Suffering, you still see seemingly hundreds of steps leading up the hillside. This is the access to the Stations of the Cross. Be aware, this way of the cross is steep and fairly arduous, but for those who are fit and healthy, it is well worth the effort. The depictions of each station are depicted in life-size (or larger) bronze sculptures. Padre Pio himself blessed the foundation stone for this Way of the Cross after he had celebrated his last-ever Mass the day before his death. In the fifth station, the sculptor has depicted Padre Pio as the Cyrenean who helps Jesus carry His Cross.

Further back from the friary, seemingly tucked away into the hillside, is the convent of the enclosed Poor Clare nuns. Construction work began on it in the Holy Year of 1975, the anniversary of Padre Pio's death, 23rd September. There is a public chapel where pilgrims can pray and attend Holy Mass.

All of the above are situated in the immediate vicinity of the friary and shrine, the area commonly referred to as The Sanctuary. In the town of San Giovanni Rotondo, and more especially various roads leading off the main road linking town and sanctuary, are to be found numerous hotels and boarding houses which accommodate pilgrims. Booking in advance is definitely advisable!

For those who have the time and the stamina, there are

several interesting churches to visit in the town of San
Giovanni Rotondo itself, such as the original church of St
John the Baptist, or the 'Rotonda', and the 15th century
chapel of Our Lady of Loreto, built by people of the
Marche region who used to come to the area on pilgrimage
to St Michael the Archangel. Of course, the town caters for
visitors with the usual souvenir shops and cafes.

For those wishing to do some quiet reading or research
for a thesis on the life and times of Saint Padre Pio, there
is a Padre Pio Reading Centre near the Sanctuary, in the
area now becoming known as the Padre Pio Citadel to
distinguish it from the nearby town. It is situated near to
the friary and the Home for the Relief of Suffering and as
well as housing almost 40,000 volumes, thousands of
pamphlets and manuscripts, as well as photographs, slides
and videocassettes, it has an exhibition of original
paintings and sculptures of Padre Pio. Opening hours are
8.30am to 1pm and 4pm to 6.30pm.

For groups arranging travel by coach, the Grotto of St
Michael the Archangel is some nine miles from San
Giovanni Rotondo. Organisers would no doubt also wish
to visit the home town of Padre Pio. At Pietrelcina, one
may visit the Padre's modest family home, the parish
church of St Anne, where he served Mass as a boy and
celebrated Mass as a young priest, the site of his first
stigmatisation in 1910 on the Piana Romana, where a
church has now been built. And there is the Capuchin

friary and church, funded mainly by Mary Pyle, which Padre Pio is said to have visited in bilocation.

Pilgrim groups flying in and out of Rome's airports and travelling by coach to and from San Giovanni Rotondo often stop *en route* to venerate the Eucharistic miracle at Lanciano. And, of course, many tie it in with a day or two in the Eternal City itself, Rome.

The endless crowds may seem ever-present at San Giovanni Rotondo. There may be much to see and do while there for only a few days. While adjusting to the presence of other cultures and languages and learning to accept others' ways of praying, there are distractions to be avoided. Those who make their way there to be inspired by the priest-saint's life and ministry may wish to keep in mind the following prayer of Pope John Paul II. Concluding his sermon at the Beatification of Padre Pio on 2nd May 1999, the Pope prayed: "May Our Lady of Grace, whom the humble Capuchin of Pietrelcina invoked with constant and tender devotion, help us to keep our gaze fixed on God. May she take us by the hand and lead us to seek wholeheartedly that supernatural charity flowing forth from the wounded side of the Crucified One."

PADRE PIO: 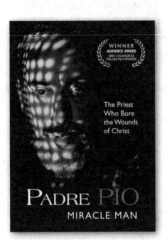 DVD
MIRACLE MAN

This movie captures the Capuchin friar's intense faith and devotion, and deep spiritual concern for others, as well as his great compassion for the sick and suffering. It reveals the amazing details and events in Padre Pio's life as a boy and throughout his 50 years as a friar, dramatizing the frequent attacks of the Devil on him, as well as the persecution he suffered at the hands of people, including those in the church. Starring Italian actor Sergio Castellitto, and directed by Carlo Carlei, this is an outstanding feature film on the amazing life of this great saint.

In Italian with English or Spanish subtitles,
or an English dubbed track.

DVD PPMM-M . . . 210 min., $24.95

ignatius press

www. ignatius.com · 1 (800) 651-1531